D1622389

style

fragrance

acknowledgements

I would like to thank Matt Handbury, Anne Wilson and Catie Ziller for the opportunity to do this book and for your continued support. I would also like to thank Anna Waddington for her endless hours of hard work and getting things organised, Marylouise Brammer for her design talent and editor Susin Chow for her attention to detail.

Special thanks to photographer Carolina Ambida for her creativity, enthusiasm and inspiration. It was a pleasure to work on this project with you.

Special thanks to my sister, Susie, for being so supportive and for spurring me on when the going got tough. I would also like to thank Stewart, Nicola, Sam and Michael for their encouragement and support. Thanks to my mum, Brenda, for her inspiration and my father, Brian, for his drive. I couldn't have got this far without you all.

Thanks for the loan of products for photography to Ruth Aran, Les Senteurs, L'Artisian Parfumeur, L'Occitane, Perfumes Isabell, Elemis, E'SPA, Guerlain, Zarvis, Jo Malone, Penhaligons, Czech & Speake, Mint, Zara Zara, Calvin Klein, Crabtree & Evelyn, Origins, Neal's Yard Remedies, Aveda, Cariad and Aromatique. Special thanks to Ghislaine Wood, Roja Dove, Sam Girdwood, Claire Lattin, Catie Briscoe, Nancy Brady and the team at Astrid Sutton Associates.

living style

fragrance

jane campsie
photography by carolina ambida

TIME
LIFE
BOOKS

contents

fragrant living

scents and sensibility

The word "perfume" comes from the Latin *per* meaning "through" and *fumus* meaning "smoke", signifying the origin of all perfumery — incense. Fragrance has been used for years in ceremonial rituals, for healing and for its beautifying benefits. The Buddhists used it religiously, Greeks valued its healing powers, Egyptian priests inhaled it to alter their minds, Indians decorated their beds with jasmine on wedding nights, and the Chinese used scents to clear oppressive atmospheres. But, most important, smells played a vital role in survival.

Initially our sense of smell was tuned for tracking enemies, loved ones, food, and sensing danger, but over time, we have had to rely less on our ability to sniff things out. Underuse, pollution, cigarette smoke, and mucus-producing diets have all dulled our sense of smell. Alarming studies suggest that the human obsession to mask body odor is leading to increased divorce rates. People we love smell good to us. We all have a signature scent, as unique as a fingerprint, which is the same only in identical twins. Produced by the apocrine glands, the substance smells similar to musk and plays a significant role in attracting our soul mate. Masking this smell interferes with our powers of attraction, and for couples having problems, it's basically obstructing a strong emotional link.

The modern world is full of aromas but most are synthetic and come from a can. It's time to rediscover natural aromas and infuse your life with pure essences that boost your well-being. Embark on a sensory journey and indulge your senses.

the sense of smell

It takes two seconds for an aroma to enter the nose and travel to the part of the brain that controls memory and emotions. Fragrance can heighten our spending capacity, improve our concentration levels, and even prompt us to settle unpaid bills. But how can a whiff of fragrance do all of this? Odor molecules pass through small nasal passages until they reach millions of olfactory sensors behind the bridge of the nose. These bind to cells that then send messages about the odor to the limbic system, the part of the brain responsible for such varied emotions as fear, rage, anger aggression, and pleasure. The limbic system also influences hormonal, metabolic, and sexual activity, as well as regulating our stress responses. This is the reason why particular fragrances have the ability to stimulate intense memories, re-create experiences, regardless of whether they were pleasant or unpleasant, and influence the way we feel and behave.

aromatherapy

It takes half a second for us to respond to a smell, compared with almost a full second to react to pain. Essential oils, extracted from plants, have been used for centuries in incense, ointments, perfumes, and lotions and potions to beautify the body. Today, they are also recognized for their emotional, spiritual, and physiological benefits. Most essential oils are made up of more than 100 constituents. Over the years, scientists have been able to isolate the active ingredients in many plants and reproduce them synthetically. Although nature-identical fragrance molecules are suitable for use in fine fragrances, they are not beneficial in aromatherapy because they do not have the same treatment properties as the pure essential oils. Therefore, when you're purchasing essential oils, always look for reputable brands that are 100 percent pure. The price of the oil is usually a good indication of its quality. Large amounts of plant material are required to produce a very small amount of oil, which makes essential oils expensive. For example, it takes 30 roses to produce just one drop of this essential oil. Cheap versions of oils will not necessarily be pure, natural essences since these scents may be synthetic or adulterated products, which may make the oils less effective.

don't turn your nose up

WOMEN HAVE a more acute sense of smell than men, and this intensifies during ovulation.

MOST ANIMALS have a more acute sense of smell than humans. Horses can smell water from a mile away, male silkworms can detect the aroma of the female species when they're 5 miles apart, and rabbits have sensory patches that equal the area of skin that covers the entire body, while a human's measures about three-quarters of a square inch.

NEVER TRY more than three fragrances at once — you'll overload your sense of smell and render yourself temporarily unable to detect new aromas.

WE HAVE the ability to detect between 5,000 and 10,000 different aromas.

IT IS believed that taking zinc tablets can help those who have lost their sense of smell.

FAMILY MEMBERS can identify one another by their scent alone.

OUR SENSE of smell is most acute between the ages of 20 and 40 and then begins to deteriorate after the age of 50.

TO NEUTRALIZE your sense of smell, inhale coffee beans.

HEAD INJURIES, exposure to pollutants, chemicals, tobacco smoke, and certain drugs can interfere with, even destroy, our sense of smell.

OUR SENSE of smell is stronger at night than in the morning.

fragrant ways

scented candles

the burning issue

Candles are a great way to infuse your surroundings with subtle aromas and emit soft light. Many commercial candles contain synthetic aromas that smell rather artificial, so buy unscented candles and lace them with fragrance yourself. Paraffin candles are naturally odorless and usually blended with stearin to keep the wax from dripping, whereas beeswax candles give off a honey aroma and are slow burning.

signature scent

To make your own, spray the outside of an unlit candle with your favorite fragrance — as the candle burns, it will gently release the aromas. Or light a candle, let it burn until a pool of wax forms, extinguish, add one or two drops of your favorite oil to the melted wax, and relight the candle. This will exude fragrance for 1 to 2 hours. Essential oils and perfumes that contain alcohol are flammable, so be careful when using these.

the right oil

For a revitalizing aroma, scent your candles with lemongrass or orange essence; for a rich, sensual fragrance, try sandalwood or cedarwood oil; and for a peaceful, tranquil ambience, try mixing chamomile and lavender essential oils. If you are burning unscented candles outdoors during the summer months, scent them with a couple of drops of lemongrass essential oil to help deter mosquitoes and other insects. To ensure that the fragrance lasts, always trim the wick of the candle so it is relatively short. When buying candles, remember those with flat tops burn less effectively than those with pointed tips. Place lighted candles on fireproof surfaces and do not leave unattended while burning. Always cup your hand around the flame before blowing it out. This will prevent the melted wax from spilling. Or you can lick the pads of your thumb and forefinger and then press over the wick to put out the flame.

burning incense

For years, incense has been burned for religious and ceremonial purposes around the world. For the best results, it's worth investing in good-quality incense sticks, cones, or coils to burn; the cheap varieties often diffuse smoky fumes and synthetic aromas. A clear glass vase becomes a decorative incense holder when filled with black sand, small pebbles, or coarse grains of sea salt to anchor the incense sticks in place. Put cones or coils in ceramic or terra-cotta dishes. As an alternative to incense, follow the ancient Indian tradition and tightly bind together dried lavender or sage sprigs with a piece of string. Light the herb bundle, then blow out the flame and leave to smolder in a ceramic dish to gently infuse your surroundings. Create your own scented sticks by filling a glass bottle with water and about 15 drops of essential oils, then stand a bundle of dried sticks or tapers in the solution. Once the ends have been impregnated with solution (after a few days), turn the sticks upside down and put the unscented ends in the bottle. The scented ends will diffuse subtle aromas into the atmosphere. The sticks should be turned regularly to release the scent and reabsorb it.

potpourri

Potpourri should be made up of interesting-looking flowers, leaves, and spices. The texture, color, and shape of the ingredients will determine how appealing and modern it looks. Hunt around for some unconventional dried herbs at Chinese herbalists or look for decorative dried spices, such as pink peppercorns and aniseed stars, which look good if you want to create a woody, earthy-looking mix. Collect berries, bits of bark, small stones, and shells to create a potpourri with a contemporary feel. When selecting ingredients, remember that scented leaves are generally more aromatic than flowers, but rose petals and lavender do retain their fragrances well. If using fresh ingredients, pick the flowers, leaves, or berries on a dry day (at least two days after any rainfall), after the dew has evaporated. Spread out the ingredients on a cotton cloth, place indoors in a dry, dark place, and allow to dry naturally. You may also use plant material that is already dried.

Place the prepared ingredients in an airtight container and mix with essential oils, allowing one drop per 2 cups of dried material. Prepare a fixative, using 1 tablespoon of orrisroot essence for every 2 to 4 cups of dried material and sprinkle over the mixture. Place a lid on the container and shake well. Store in a dry, dark, warm place for six weeks and shake regularly to blend the ingredients.

If potpourri is placed in a bowl, stir it regularly to release the fragrance. The scent of potpourri needs reviving every 2 to 3 months. Place the mixture in an airtight container, add a few drops of essential oils, shake well, and leave overnight. Or sprinkle a few drops of essential oil directly into the bowl of potpourri and stir well. In place of traditional potpourri, try draping bundles of scented pine cones on the radiators, ceiling, banisters, mantelpiece, or dining table. To enhance the natural aroma of the cones, simply soak them overnight in 5 oz (150 ml) of water and 25 drops of pine essential oil. Let dry before using. Avoid placing either potpourri or pine cones near open flames; some of the ingredients are flammable.

vaporizing oils

oil burner

Vaporizing aromatic essences is one of the simplest and easiest ways to scent your surroundings and purify the air. There are three main types of burners for vaporizing essences. Usually made from metal, earthenware, or porcelain, traditional burners are heated by a candle and vaporize a mixture of water and essential oils. The main drawback with this type of burner is if the water has evaporated and the oils continue to burn, it creates a black, sticky residue that can be hard to remove. Electric diffusers usually vaporize neat essential oils and are safer to be left unattended than candle-fueled burners. Steam diffusers use a cold-air pump to blow minuscule essential oil droplets into the atmosphere but are costly.

To scent a room, use between 4 and 10 drops of essential oils (diluted with water, depending on the type of burner you have). Start with a few drops and gauge how intense the aroma is.

suitable choice

Lavender and chamomile essential oils have soothing, tranquilizing properties, while lime, lemon, and bergamot can be used to uplift. To instill a sensuous ambience, burn rose and geranium. To cleanse a sick room, burn lavender or tea tree oil. When cleaning the surfaces of oil burners, let them cool down and then wipe with a cloth. Sticky oil residues can be removed with a small amount of rubbing alcohol and then wiped clean with water.

ring burner

Heavy-duty plastic, cardboard, and ceramic fragrant rings fit on top of a light bulb and are an alternative to oil burners for scenting your surroundings. Drop aromatherapy essences on the rim of the ring with a little water and as the bulb heats up, the vapors evaporate. To clean a ring burner, wipe with rubbing alcohol and then wash with hot water to remove all traces of the alcohol.

room sprays

Fragrant sprays will instantly banish unpleasant aromas, enliven the senses and, during warm weather, can lower room temperatures by displacing heat particles. To make your own room spray, mix 10 drops of your chosen essential oil with 10 oz (300 ml) warm water in a clean spray bottle. Shake well and then spritz in rooms. Avoid spraying near wooden objects or furniture and antique surfaces, as the water can interfere with their finishes. Or try adding aromatic ingredients, such as cinnamon sticks, vanilla beans, or fresh verbena leaves, to near-boiling water, steep for 20 minutes and then strain the liquid before storing in a spray bottle. To banish the odors of pets, try using a citronella or lemongrass room spray (both oils are also reputed to repel fleas and ticks); to remove stale odors from rooms, opt for an antiseptic blend of tea tree, eucalyptus, thyme, lavender, and lemongrass; and to counteract unpleasant kitchen smells, try mixing lime and lemon essential oils with water. All of these room sprays can also be used to vaporize in oil burners.

fresh flowers

Plants and flowers perfume the air and act as humidifiers, refreshing our surroundings and environment. When cutting flowers from the garden, always try to pick them in the mornings or late in the day — if you pick them when the sun is high, they are more likely to wilt. Stand them in tepid water immediately after picking and cut the stems at an angle before arranging — this ensures that the stems absorb the maximum amount of water to survive longer. Lilacs, Madonna lilies, narcissuses, and tuberoses give off heady aromas and so are suitable to display in large rooms or in a mixed arrangement with foliage and other unscented flowers. Roses have a less intrusive aroma and work well on their own.

House plants bring color to your home but also help purify the air. Not only do green plants absorb the carbon dioxide we expel, transforming it into oxygen, but *Allaomena* and *Syndonium* take up benzene fumes and philodendrons and spider plants extract large amounts of formaldehyde from the atmosphere. Peruvian cactus, *Cereus uruguayanus*, has white, scented flowers and helps reduce electromagnetic pollution from computers and televisions. Fragrant, easy-care flowering plants to bring indoors for a few days include hyacinths, freesias, gardenias, violets, jasmine, narcissuses, and lilies. Don't put them next to other fragrant objects, and be careful with very potent plants that can overpower in small, warm rooms.

floral scenting

Taking your pick of the seasonal
scents that flowers and plants exude.

summer roses, dianthus, honeysuckle, frangipani, lavender, lilies, tuberoses,
passion flower, Virginian stocks

spring freesias, hyacinths, jonquils, evening primrose,
violets, lily of the valley, wisteria, sweet peas

autumn belladonna lily, nicotiana, cyclamen, heliotrope, clematis, roses

winter daphne, mimosa, winter jasmine, christmas rose, viburnum, witch hazel, winter iris

aromatic living

the scented ambience

Surround yourself with fragrance to indulge your senses and enhance the appeal of your home. Always ensure that fresh air circulates freely around the rooms and then scent your world with natural aromatherapy essences.

Research has shown that the environment inside our homes can be 10 times more toxic than the outside world. Advanced technology means it is possible to synthetically re-create the smell of practically any substance. In our quest for hygiene and cleanliness, we are using so many synthetic aromas to mask environmental smells that our houses are actually being polluted with the chemicals found in detergents, air fresheners, and cleaning products.

Take the natural route to healthy living and use only pure essential oils to protect, preserve, and heighten the pleasure of your world. Essential oils will have a positive effect on the way you feel and can help preserve and protect your possessions. Unlike the synthetic aromas, many of these essences have antibacterial and antifungal properties.

aromatic living

the hall

Hallways and the entrances to your home should be scented with aromas of geranium and lavender oils, which will make guests feel at ease. Citrus oils are also a good choice as they are not too overpowering. As an alternative to vaporizing essences, place scented sachets under rugs or concoct natural room sprays and spritz onto carpets regularly. The rugs and carpets will gently release the fragrance as they are trodden on. If using fresh flowers to scent a large hallway or entrance lobby, opt for heady, scented blooms such as lilacs, tuberoses, or narcissuses. Use bold colors and interesting-shaped flowers and foliage to make an impact, but make sure your arrangements won't keep people from passing. If hallways are dark and drafty, fragrant house plants are not a suitable choice.

the living room

Your living room should be scented with essences that evoke warm and welcoming feelings, especially during the cold weather. Try burning essences of orange, sandalwood, and geranium or a more warming blend of amber, musk, vanilla, and frankincense. When temperatures rise, vaporize cooling essences of lemon, lime, and grapefruit or sprinkle plant-based waters and eau de cologne onto the fabrics and furnishings, which will mask any musky smells that often accompany the heat. If there is a lingering smell of cigarette or cigar smoke once your guests have left, concoct a powerful room spray. Mix 5 drops of thyme oil, 12 drops of rosemary, and 8 drops of pine essence in 4 oz (125 ml) water. Place in a spray bottle, shake well, and spritz through the room and on the rug.

aromatic living

the kitchen

The kitchen generates a wealth of aromas, from the mouth-watering smell of freshly baked bread to the pungent odors of hard-boiled eggs and burned toast. To counteract these unpleasant kitchen smells, pine and eucalyptus essential oils will deodorize and thyme and rosemary will disinfect. Room sprays with essential oils of lemon and lime leave you with a clean-smelling, fragrant room, but they also help banish the tiny fat molecules that are released into the air during roasting, frying, or grilling foods. The scent molecules of these essential oils encapsulate the fat molecules and disperse them.

cleansing agents

To maintain hygiene levels and destroy bacteria, eucalyptus oil comes into its own. The disinfecting properties of this essence actually improve with age, so if you have a bottle of eucalyptus oil that is past its shelf life for use on the face or body, put a drop down the sink or use on a cloth while cleaning.

fragrant surroundings

Fresh potted herbs, such as rosemary, thyme, and basil, can be placed on windowsills to help scent your kitchen.

culinary delights

You can use culinary ingredients such as whole dried cloves, juniper berries, ginger, black pepper, and orange peel in a vaporizer to scent your surroundings. Place a teaspoon of ingredients in the water bowl of a tea-light candle vaporizer and fill with water, or use orange or rosewater for added effect. To intensify the aroma, add half a teaspoon of sugar to the water. Within an hour, the fragrance will be released. Other culinary aromas that are reputed to affect the way we feel include chocolate, which is supposed to have a calming effect on the brain, and bananas, green apples, and peppermint, which have odors that can suppress hunger pangs. Scientists suspect the sense of smell may both dull the appetite and trick the brain into thinking food has been eaten.

aromatic living

dining room

Keep room scents subtle in your dining area, otherwise the smells of food, wine, and fragrance can become overpowering while eating. For subtle scenting, burn beeswax candles, which exude a honey scent, or place fresh fragrant flowers on the table. Roses and lilies are good choices since they emit subtle scents. If you want to vaporize oils, opt for neroli, jasmine, or rose.

right ambience

Try burning one drop each of clove, mandarin, and sweet marjoram oils when entertaining. It's a recipe for a successful evening because it makes guests feel at ease, but it also encourages a social atmosphere. Geranium oil also creates a relaxed atmosphere and clary sage encourages conversation and is slightly euphoric. For a romantic dinner, spice up the room with essences of jasmine, patchouli, and ylang-ylang.

fragrant work

Add finishing touches to each place setting with a scattering of fragrant petals or a bundle of cinnamon sticks. When filling water pitchers, add sprigs of lemon balm or make ice cubes with rose or violet petals. Use fresh lemon verbena leaves or sprigs of rosemary to scent finger bowls.

aromatic living

the bedroom

Bedrooms should be well ventilated and cooler than other rooms in your home. Overheated, stuffy rooms can leave you feeling drained and akin to being hungover when you wake up. Surround yourself with calming scents of jasmine, camomile, rose, ylang-ylang and neroli. Plants that release perfume in the evening, such as honeysuckle, evening primrose, and moonflowers, should be grown close to the bedroom window, or look for plants that are active at night, such as orchids and aloe vera. If you have trouble sleeping, sprinkle a few drops of lavender oil onto your pillow or bring a lavender plant into the room at night. The essence is reputed to have a calming effect and to help promote peaceful sleep.

the bathroom

The bathroom has become a haven for rest and relaxation. To reap the benefits and instill a sense of tranquillity, scent the bathroom with soothing essences of lavender, chamomile, rose, or jasmine. An aromatherapy bath will scent the room and is also one of the quickest ways to absorb the benefits of these essences into the bloodstream. For an invigorating wake-up experience, open the bathroom windows, maximize the amount of natural light in the room, and surround yourself with uplifting essences of grapefruit, lemon, and bergamot. Use scented candles at night — in addition to the fragrance factor, they are much more pleasant than harsh electric lighting. Always avoid using electric vaporizers in the bathroom.

fragrant ways

For quick and easy scenting, try adding a few drops of your favorite essential oil to the cardboard on the inside of a toilet-paper roll. As the roll is used, it will release the fragrant aroma. When cleaning the bathroom, place a drop of either lemon, grapefruit, bergamot, or orange oil onto a damp cloth and use to wipe over surfaces. This will deodorize without leaving a strong smell. Also, the essences of thyme, eucalyptus, pine, sage, rosemary, and tea tree have strong disinfectant properties.

aromatic living

the office

For many years, the Japanese have been vaporizing essential oils through office air-conditioning systems to improve the performance of employees. In the morning, energizing essences help stimulate productivity; after lunch, certain scents are used to combat drowsiness; and before quitting time, relaxing aromas are used to help employees unwind. Work places should be scented with essences that heighten concentration, creativity, and productivity.

mood enhancers

To enhance creativity, try burning bergamot, lemon, or geranium oil. To boost concentration, take a whiff of lemongrass oil. Studies in Japan show that computer users made 53 percent fewer errors when their work environment was infused with lemon essence.

To overcome feelings of burnout, try vaporizing essences of jasmine and lavender. When the pressure is on, calm frayed nerves by taking a whiff of vanilla and then relax your breathing by inhaling deeply through the nose and exhaling slowly through the mouth.

healthy living

To create a healthy work environment, make sure that fresh air circulates through your office and place ionizers near electrical equipment. Surround yourself with fresh flowers: They will help keep spirits high and can cut down on pollutants. For example, tulips can remove nasties such as xylene found in computer screens. Place living plants around you to help to purify the air, add moisture to the atmosphere, and disperse pollutants such as computer emissions.

aromatic living

infant's room

Babies can identify their mothers by their sense of smell alone. Within three days of being born, an infant will have made an olfactory bond with its mother. This is why certain aromas can offer us comfort. Consult your pediatrician before using aromatherapy in your infant's room. When vaporizing essential oils in an infant's room, it's advisable to dilute the oils with one tablespoon of water as some essences can easily overpower small human beings. Or you can place a bowl of steaming water in the room, out of the infant's reach, add one drop of essential oil, and agitate the water to release the aromas. If a baby is suffering from digestive problems — such as regurgitation, colic, indigestion, constipation, or diarrhea — use dill oil (it is the active ingredient used in many baby preparations for digestive conditions); if your baby is having trouble sleeping, try using chamomile oil; and if you want to make the room smell pleasant, opt for lavender oil.

children's rooms

As children grow up, you can introduce aromatherapy into their lives, but essential oils can be very powerful so it is important to seek advice from a qualified aromatherapist and medical professional or work on the basis of using half the doses normally recommended for adults. A child's room should be stimulating and tactile, with color, texture, and smell. Find ways to infuse a child's environment with aromas — tie cinnamon sticks together with brightly colored ribbons or slip scented sachets into pillows or under rugs. If your child has a tendency to be hyperactive, vaporize a calming blend of one drop each of chamomile, lavender, and lemon oils mixed with a teaspoon of water. Plug-in electric burners or steam vaporizers are the safest options for children's rooms. For teenagers who dislike cleaning and rarely open windows to air their rooms, burn essences of lavender or tea tree; both deodorize and disinfect.

fragrant innovations

fragrant innovations

book work

If you want to scent your books or wish to mask the musty smell of old journals, spray pieces of blotting paper with fragrance and place in between the pages. To help preserve the paper, try lavender or cedarwood essential oils. Use a sprig of rosemary or a fragrant leaf or flower as a bookmark.

fragrant cushions

Fill sachets with dried herbs and flowers, such as lavender and rose petals, and then place the fragrant sachets inside pillow covers. Every time someone touches the pillow, it will release the aroma.

scented curtains

To subtly perfume your room, add 6 to 10 drops of an essential oil or fragrance to a handkerchief or cotton ball and then place one in the lining of each curtain. Every time you draw the curtains, you will release the aromas. Refresh the fragrance once a month with additional drops of oil.

clothing sense

To leave your underwear, sweaters, and clothing delicately scented, spray them with your favorite perfume or add a few drops of your favorite essential oil to a cotton handkerchief and put it in your closet or drawers.

fragrant innovations

cupboard creations

To scent cupboards and drawers with fragrance, wrap a bundle of cinnamon sticks together with ribbon and place it among your belongings or fill a muslin bag with dried cloves, lemongrass, or lavender sprigs. Or you could spray some blotting or lining paper with your favorite fragrance, brush over the paper with orrisroot powder to fix the scent, and use to line the shelves or drawers.

To help keep moths at bay, opt for lavender or cedarwood essential oils.

ironing ease

Essential oils are not water soluble, so they should not be added to the water compartment of your iron; they will leave a residue. To give your clothes a subtle aroma while ironing, add a few drops of lavender, neroli, rose, or jasmine essential oil to a filled water spray, shake well, and lightly mist the clothes before ironing. If you're pressing garments that will not be worn for a while, it's advisable to use a spray with cedarwood to help protect and preserve the clothes.

fragrant innovations

scented laundry

Add 3 to 5 drops of your favorite essential oils at the fabric softener stage of your washing machine's cycle to scent your clothes with a subtle aroma. When washing bed linen, use chamomile oil to help you sleep better, and if you are suffering from a cold, opt for eucalyptus or rosemary oil. When washing by hand, add two drops of essential oil to the water during the final rinse. To scent garments in the dryer, sprinkle a couple of drops of essential oil onto a cotton handkerchief and put this in the dryer. This will scent both your clothes and laundry room.

fragrant waters

Many commercial dishwashing liquids are doused with synthetic fragrances, so buy the unscented varieties and then perfume the detergent yourself with a few drops of either lemongrass, pine, or eucalyptus essential oils. Shake well before using. If you hate washing the dishes, these essential oils can have a positive effect on the way you feel. Or try adding a few sprigs of rosemary or thyme to the bottle of liquid to help infuse the detergent with pleasant aromas and to improve its cleansing properties. Rinse dishes thoroughly.

fragrant innovations

cleaning solutions

If streaky marks remain after you've cleaned your windows, place a couple of drops of lime, lemon, or grapefruit oil on a piece of old newspaper and use it to buff the windows. The newspaper will remove any marks and when the sunshine warms the glass, the oil will release a fresh, zesty aroma. To clean copper ware, put one drop of lemon oil on a soft cloth and use to buff. When washing the paintwork in your home or office, infuse hot soapy water with a couple of drops of eucalyptus, lemon, lime, or lavender essential oil.

carpet freshener

To remove stale odors from rugs, mix 3 1/2 oz (100 g) of bicarbonate of soda with 20 drops of essential oil in a plastic container, seal, and leave overnight. Sprinkle liberally over the carpet, wait 10 minutes, and vacuum. It's a natural alternative to chemical rug cleaners. Use a different scented solution each season to freshen up your carpet and make your rooms smell good. Opt for floral fragrances in spring; zesty essences in summer; warm, spicy aromas in the autumn; and rich, woody scents in the winter.

fragrant innovations

perfect ambience

To effortlessly scent your surroundings during the cold winter months, place a couple of drops of either eucalyptus, pine, sandalwood, or patchouli essential oil on a cotton ball and put it behind the radiator. Replace the cotton ball every two weeks with a freshly scented piece.

room scent

Sprinkle a couple of drops of perfume or essential oil onto a light bulb before turning it on. As the bulb heats up, the fragrant essence will evaporate.

aromatic burning

If you have an open fire, add one drop of either cypress, pine, sandalwood, or cedarwood oil to each log, leave for 30 minutes, and then put the wood on the fire. Essential oils are flammable, so don't drop them directly onto burning logs. One scented log will be sufficient for each fire. Or when the fire has died down, add sprigs of dried lavender, sage or lemon verbena to the glowing embers to create a pleasant aroma. To get rid of food smells from a barbecue, place a couple of sprigs of rosemary on the smoldering coals.

aroma-psychology

mood enhancing

Aroma-psychology uses essential oils to positively influence the state of mind and determine our behavior. Throughout history, fragrances have been used to tap into the human subconscious to determine everything from our spending habits to our work performance.

Hospitals have successfully weaned patients off chemical tranquilizers by vaporizing lavender into the environment (the scent has a calming effect on the brain). Supermarkets have long been diffusing aromas of fresh baked goods to tempt our taste buds and encourage us to buy more. Now, airports are toying with the idea of releasing calming essences into departure lounges to help passengers with preflight anxiety, and fashion designers are looking into branding garments with specific smells to put a stop to knockoffs. Research is also underway to create special vaporizing systems in cars that will release energizing essences to prevent drivers from falling asleep on long journeys.

Because fragrances can tap into the subconscious and therefore influence the way we feel and behave, it makes sense to use natural essential oils and fragrances in our homes and surroundings to enhance our positive moods and counteract negative emotions.

fragrant moods

angry & agitated

Repressed anger can manifest itself in conditions ranging from chronic fatigue, backaches, and skin disorders to an inability to concentrate. Use calming essences of chamomile, tuberose, linden blossom, vetiver, and lavender to disperse feelings of fury. Also, you should try this quick colour-therapy treatment — simply focus on a piece of blue paper or a blue object for two minutes. This will have a calming effect on the mind and helps lower blood pressure, heart rate, and respiration.

tense & overactive

To calm an overactive mind, try inhaling or vaporizing lavender essential oil; it has a sedating effect on the brain. Also, take time out to relax. Research has shown 10 minutes of proper relaxation can leave you feeling as refreshed as if you've had a good night's sleep.

drained & burned out

If you're mentally and physically exhausted, take a warm bath scented with a couple of drops of lavender oil and then go to bed. Sleep is one of the best antidotes for restoring your health. If you need a pick-me-up, energizing essences of grapefruit, lemon, and peppermint will come to the rescue. Don't use peppermint oil if you are taking homeopathic remedies; mint has an antidote effect.

distressed & upset

If you've been through a trying time, the best solution is to surround yourself with comforting smells. Dilute 5 drops each of rose and neroli oils and 15 drops of mandarin oil in 1 1/2 oz (40 ml) of base oil. Put 8 drops in the bath or in a burner. Exercising will also help lift anxiety, but opt for low-intensity activity. If you work out too hard, it will only make you more anxious and distraught.

fragrant moods

unbalanced & low

If you're feeling under the weather, try vaporizing uplifting essential oils of mandarin, chamomile, lemon, bergamot, grapefruit, and orange. To boost your spirits, eat foods rich in serotonin, such as bananas, cantaloupe, and pineapples. Serotonin is a substance created by the body to enhance feel-good sensations and it is also present in these foods.

tired & irritated

To rebalance your mind, body, and spirit, mix 15 drops of ylang-ylang, 10 drops of coriander, and 5 of chamomile oil in 2 oz (60 ml) of base oil and add 5 drops of the mixture to the bath or use in an oil burner. If you wake up in the morning feeling grouchy, it could be due to an overload of acidic wastes in the body. To counteract, drink a glass of hot water with the juice of half a lemon.

restless & anxious

Throw a few chamomile tea bags into the bathtub while the water is running. Let it steep, remove, and then relax in the tub for 10 minutes. Before taking a bath, clear thoughts from your mind by writing a list of your troubles. Relax in the bath in a meditative state.

bored & unfocused

If you're feeling unsettled and you're finding it hard to focus on things, give yourself a massage using a blend of 2 oz (60 ml) of base oil with 5 drops each of thyme and rosemary essential oils, 6 drops of lemon, and 4 drops of basil. Also, try meditation or yoga.

instant mood enhancers

IF YOU'RE suffering from mental fatigue, add a couple of drops of peppermint oil to a handkerchief and inhale deeply.

TO BOOST energy levels, vaporize zesty citrus oils of orange, grapefruit, lemon, or lime. Avoid warm-smelling fragrances since they hamper activity.

TO COUNTERACT the effects of low self-esteem and insecurity, opt for soft floral scents or essences of jasmine, ylang-ylang, and geranium.

WHEN YOUR spirits are flagging, rosemary and eucalyptus essential oils will come to the rescue.

TO IMPROVE assertiveness, essential oils of jasmine, basil, cedarwood, and ylang-ylang will be beneficial.

IF YOU are suffering from nervous exhaustion, a combination of lavender and jasmine essential oils will help restore your natural balance.

IF YOU'RE feeling sad and anxious, try vaporizing patchouli or geranium oil; they are reputed to be both grounding and stimulating.

TO BOOST feelings of contentment, rose, cypress, and lavender will come into their own.

making sense

fragrant solutions

perfume tips

If you spray perfume on your wrists, never rub them together afterward because you will dull the development of the fragrance's extracts. Never spray perfume onto fur, jewelry (especially pearls and gilt items), or delicate clothes (particularly items made from synthetic fabrics), since it can damage them.

the right spirit

Before filling a perfume atomizer with a new fragrance, always remove all traces of the existing aroma. For the best results, rinse with pure vodka, then water, and allow to dry.

test run

To try a new perfume, spray on your wrists and wait for 10 to 15 minutes before you decide to make a purchase. Never test new fragrances on paper; they need to react with the chemicals released by your skin for you to experience how they truly smell.

fragrance alternatives

If wearing perfumes irritates your skin, try spritzing a fine, fragrant mist through your hair before blow-drying. You can also spray the fragrance onto your hairbrush and then comb the scent through your hair.

fragrant solutions

blending oils

Essential oils (with the exception of lavender and tea tree oil) should not be applied neat to the skin. Always blend essential oils with a base or carrier oil, such as sweet almond, jojoba, olive, carrot, sesame, or avocado. For bathing, you can add essential oils directly to the bath water, but since these plant essences are quite strong, either mix them with a carrier oil or add a tablespoon of milk to the water.

For massage, use a ratio of 10 drops of essential oil to 1 oz (30 ml) of base oil. For room sprays and oil burners, dilute the oils with tap water.

aromatherapy oils

Always stick to the recommended doses — if you overuse essences, they can have the opposite effect of the one you are after. For example, lavender is a known relaxant but used in abundance, it has a stimulating effect. Never use oils in place of medication prescribed by a doctor and always keep them out of reach of children. If using essential oils for children, halve the doses that are recommended for adults and always dilute with a base oil. Consult a qualified aromatherapist before using essential oils if you are pregnant, epileptic, or have high blood pressure.

fragrant solutions

fragrance findings

Research suggests that people who regularly wear fragrance have a more positive outlook on socializing and may be more socially skilled than those who seldom or never wear it. If others think you smell good, you will have more confidence.

In studies, introverts have shown they prefer spicy fragrances, extroverts favor fresh, green, floral fragrances, and the dreamy types are drawn to floral, powdery scents.

wearing perfume

Apply perfume to your pulse points (scientists have located 16 on the body including on the inside of the wrists, the cleavage, the temples, and the back of the knees). Contrary to popular belief, you should not dab fragrance behind your ears; numerous oil glands there can interfere with the scent. Instead, dab on the neck or the side of the throat about 3 in (8 cm) below the ears.

changing scents

The same fragrance can smell different depending on who is wearing it. Body temperature, medication, nutrition, smoking, and hormonal changes can influence how a fragrance smells on the skin. These underlying factors prompt the release of chemicals, through the skin, that then interact with the scent molecules and alter how they smell on an individual. This explains why a fragrance you usually wear can smell different from time to time. The brain stops registering a smell after about 15 minutes, so it's hardly surprising that if you wear the same perfume day in, day out, you won't be able to detect it.

fresh air

Stagnant air can be a breeding ground for bacteria so open the windows to ensure that the air doesn't become stale, and burn lavender or tea tree essential oil — both of these have antibacterial properties.

fragrant solutions

seasonal scents

Scent your surroundings to suit the seasons. This will instantly liberate your senses and prepare you for the season ahead. As spring arrives, it's advisable to scent your home with delicate floral essences of jasmine, neroli, and ylang-ylang; when summer sets in, enjoy the smell of fresh-cut grass, sea breezes, or zesty, citrus aromas; for autumn, choose warm, spicy accords of cinnamon, ginger, and juniper; and during winter, infuse your home with the sensuous aromas of sandalwood, patchouli, myrrh, and cedarwood to help beat the cold weather blues. Celebrate the festive season with essences of clove, mandarin, pine, cinnamon, ginger, or orange.

storage tips

Keeping essential oils and perfumes away from sunlight and heat will help preserve their shelf life. Store essential oils in dry, cool places, preferably in their boxes. An opened bottle of most oils will last up to 12 months; citrus oils have the shortest shelf life, roughly 6 months. Unopened bottles of fragrance, if stored properly, should keep safely for up to three years. A perfume bottle, once opened, will last up to 18 months. You can tell if an essential oil or fragrance has gone bad when the liquid changes color, the consistency thickens, or it smells funny. Aromatherapy oils and blends should be kept in dark-colored glass bottles to best preserve them.

TIME LIFE BOOKS

Published by Time-Life Books, a division of Time Life Inc.
Time-Life is a trademark of Time Warner Inc. and affiliated companies.

Time-Life Books
Vice President and Publisher: Neil S. Levin
Vice President, Content Development: Jennifer L. Pearce
Senior Sales Director: Richard J. Vreeland
Director, Marketing and Publicity: Inger Forland
Director of New Product Development: Carolyn M. Clark
Director of Custom Publishing: John Lalor
Director of Rights and Licensing: Olga Vezeris
Executive Editor: Linda Bellamy
Director of Design: Tina Taylor

First published in 2000 by Murdoch Books®,
a division of Murdoch Magazines Pty Ltd,
GPO Box 1203, Sydney, NSW Australia 2001

Photographer: Carolina Ambida
Creative Director/Stylist: Jane Campsie
Concept and Design: Marylouise Brammer
Project Manager: Anna Waddington
Editor: Susin Chow

Group General Manager: Mark Smith
Publisher: Kay Scarlett
Production Manager: Liz Fitzgerald

Library of Congress Cataloging-in-Publication Data available upon request.
ISBN 0-7370-3028-3

Printed by Toppan Printing Hong Kong Co. Ltd.
PRINTED IN CHINA. This edition printed 2001.